THE
TONGUES
OF
EARTH

MARK ABLEY

bitlit

A **free** eBook edition is available
with the purchase of this print book.

CLEARLY PRINT YOUR NAME ABOVE IN UPPER CASE

Instructions to claim your free eBook edition:
1. Download the BitLit app for Android or iOS
2. Write your name in **UPPER CASE** on the line
3. Use the BitLit app to submit a photo
4. Download your eBook to any device

COTEAU
BOOKS

www.coteaubooks.com

THE
TONGUES
OF
EARTH

MARK ABLEY

Edited by Liz Philips
Cover design by Scott Hunter
Typeset by Susan Buck
Printed and bound in Canada

Library and Archives Canada Cataloguing in Publication

Abley, Mark, 1955-, author
    The tongues of earth / Mark Abley.

Poems.
Issued in print and electronic formats.
ISBN 978-1-55050-610-5 (pbk.).--ISBN 978-1-55050-611-2 (pdf)

    I. Title.

PS8551.B45T66 2015   C811'.54   C2014-907371-2
                                          C2014-907372-0

2517 Victoria Avenue
Regina, Saskatchewan
Canada S4P 0T2
www.coteaubooks.com

Available in Canada from:
Publishers Group Canada
2440 Viking Way
Richmond, British Columbia
Canada V6V 1N2

10 9 8 7 6 5 4 3 2

Coteau Books gratefully acknowledges the financial support of its publishing program by: the Saskatchewan Arts Board, The Canada Council for the Arts, the Government of Canada through the Canada Book Fund, the City of Regina, and the Government of Saskatchewan through Creative Saskatchewan.

For Annie
For Kayden
For Megan

Table of Contents

PART
ONE

As If

somewhere on the
    tidal earth, the traffic
        gone, arrives an hour
when, a cat persistent and
    plaintive at the door,

    you stumble out of
bed to let her in
    and, as she brushes
        your ankles in a cool
wave of night-scented air,

    hear a bird on a scarcely
        discernible branch
of a high ash
    by the road begin to try
        out his pair of songstruck

lungs – tentative,
    explorative – as if
        any god worth his salt
would create
    music before light

Chauvet

don't look for any   pictures of everyday life
chiselled or smudged on limestone   and spared by water
that drips from our own   time into death's private cave
no portraits, no self-portraits   no ice-chewed landscapes
or charts of the night   domesticating the stars
no hint of Neanderthals
                                    nothing a painter
could have heard or seen   in a conifer valley
except the spirit bodies   who would give their flesh
to a loving spear
                            and become these agile shapes
populating a rockface   as if rough torches
and crafty fingers   had summoned them onto walls
to watch the humans, to watch   ourselves: musk oxen
bison pursued by   a pride of maneless lions
rhinos hornlocked in battle   a cave bear scenting
a cowed hyena   mammoths with no conception
their future will stop
                            this cornucopia
a silent archive   a gallery of desire
its beloved images   feared, worshipped, slaughtered
fallen out of mind   driven beyond memory
unbreathing and unmoving
                                    but for the horses
still whinnying now
                            and the blood-coloured handprints

Mark Abley

Labrador

A gravel road to the sea.
A raw wind. The end of a world.

A pile of scanty earth heaped with rocks.

Under the pile, just off the road, the skeleton
of a boy buried face down, a flat
stone across his lower back,
and to give him hope on his journey
a walrus tusk, reddened pebbles, a flute
sculpted from a bird's bone
and the toggled point of a harpoon.

A deserted beach, the morning after rain,
sliced by a stream through the sand.

Fragments of a warship near a lighthouse
the colour of ice beyond
a village of seven.
                    Seven thousand
years ago, who wrapped his body
in bark and animal skins
and placed his head toward the falling sun?
Who lit the fires beside him and cooked food?

No bowheads offshore. No walruses.
No smoke curling over the valley.
The end of a world. A raw wind.

A sandpiper's tracks along the shore.

Birth

You know who's waiting nearby.
Night's cloak and a pale horse.
The glint of a sharpened sickle. The crackle
of bone without flesh. We try
anything, everything to elude
his gaze.
        Strange if we never
recall his long-lost twin, his favourite
enemy, his silent partner. Did we
glimpse her when the dark sky
opened? Did we notice her sure touch
on that earbreaking rush
down to light and the gulped hiss
of air?
        Does nobody remember her?
An after-image on a retina.
The dream that comforts a patient gasping
in a pink-walled room, wired
and tubed, clamped in place, lips like
hard sand, to the tick
of machines:
        A red-haired dancer
in a green dress, her hands outstretched
to the sun. Or a Rift Valley Eve.
Or a smiling child looking up from
a game of shells and stepping over
the bare floor of a brushwood
hut where rice is boiling
to hold a curtain wide, saying
        Don't
worry. Don't be afraid.

Forget Me Not

Before the sea grew, the elders say,
there were villages and farms edging out from
what's now the shore, and the seals who turn
whiskered heads in the air to watch
people on the kelp-entangled rocks can dive
among houses where the fish slip through doorways
or hide in jumbles of fallen slate.

And once, before the sea grew, a boy who lived
in such a village came running home to show
his mother a pair of eggs he found by a wall,
eggs the colour of forget-me-nots, as cool
to his touch as a shadowed stone on a hill
that welcomes, even now, the flight of larks and hawks
and sunlight unhampered by water.

"Don't worry," she told him, "they were never meant
to hatch." But he cradled them, one in each hand,
up a rough path overlooking the bay
and lodged them in a swirl of hazel. That morning
the village quivered in a dry breeze
that quickened the passage of small boats and no-one,
the elders say, imagined the future.

The Almost Island

                    Rising
and rising as the planet's crust
buckles and two continents shuffle closer,
inching up like a secret Ararat from
a ridge on the ocean's turbulent floor
through miles of lightening water, each crag
within view of the surface explored by dolphins
and sharks, reconnoitred by petrels:
immune to the force of rain and fog:
all prepared for some radiant Thursday morning
when the sea recedes with grudging compliance
from a peak that has become dry land.

Not yet, not for us, though gossip tells
how the wide-eyed crew of a Japanese trawler
rescued a woman from Buenos Aires
who had walked off a yacht after midnight:
imagine her shock as she found herself, not
in the airless depths but chest-high in chilly water,
balancing on a hidden summit. "Am I dead
already?" she asked the black waves; and as if
in response, a long-submerged craving for life
poured over her like a passion for mangoes –
their texture, their flavour, their unpredictable
sweetness.

White on White

Energy is Eternal Delight, said Mr. Blake

now I face a February morning by a lake
below a gull at work in the delighted air

as the wet snow settles, flake by flake,
onto melting ridges that sketch a line of jagged
puddles in the churning, half-solid water

soon, I think, the weather will have to break
but soon means nothing to this granite wind
or the dour, unbroken mass of clouds transforming
the far shore to a moist abstraction

luckily the mirrored pier declines to fall
though its legs look akilter, a cubist slush pile,
ice and former ice in a cracked reflection

a watercolour still life that keeps on shifting
while a frozen artist tries to freeze the action

and the ghost of Mr. Blake cries satisfaction

Deep Gold

(adapted from the journals and letters of Samuel Palmer, 1805–1881)

1823

I feel, ten minutes of the day, the most
Ardent love for art, and lose the rest
Of time in this restless despondency,
A blind and listless apathy, without
Any of those delicious visions, the great
Joys of my life – the Saviour at Emmaus,
A thief repenting on the cross, the promise
Made to our father Abraham, and several
Glimpses of a world of chivalry,
Mellowed with deep gold to discriminate
Against our flashy and distracted days.

1824

The sweet encouragement he granted me
(For Christ blessed little children) did not lead
To lazy arrogance, but made me work
Harder and better that afternoon and night.
A vision of the scene possesses me:
In this corrupt, genteelly stupid town
My spirit sees his home (the chariot
Of the sun) as an island in a tarnished sea,
So rich is it in primitive grandeur –
Whether in the forms of Mr. and Mrs. Blake
Or in the items hanging on the walls.

1828

Creation sometimes pours into the eye
The radiance of Heaven: green mountains
That shimmer in a summer twilight as
The western valleys fade – the moon, opening
Her golden eye, or voyaging through shoals
Of light – not only thrill the optic nerve
But shed a grateful, calm, unearthly lustre
To penetrate the inmost spirits. I
Believe this realm to be the veil of Heaven,
The setting of our table for a feast:
A dream of eternity, the antepast.

1835

These wretched days of poverty have wiped
The bloom from all my summer splendour.
Consigned to the dumps, I labour there in vain
As if I, alone of all mankind, were doomed
To get no bread by the sweat of my brow –
If there's a mangy cat you want to drown
Christen it *Palmer*. Can you grant a loan?
Three pounds will bring me safe to London, where
I'll sell my ancient books and paint the sun,
The moon and Milky Way on drinking signs…
The candle's burning out, my friend. Goodbye.

1838

Duty is difficult, and nothing, up
From blacking shoes, is easily done well:
At thirty the illusions drop away.
This searching of heart, to see if I'm a fool
In grain, has darkened every night since May
And I long to feel a blade of sunlight break
My winter crust. Does no-one taste the golden
Autumn of life? We are green first, then grey;
And then we're nothing in this world, and as far
Removed from the succeeding generation
As the busy men and women of Pompeii.

1859

I felt, while the rain was billowing last night,
The refreshment I suppose a plant would gain
Under that lively influence after drought.
I dread the dust of town — it withers me —
And would prefer, could I but have my will,
A month's incessant rain. What a mockery
To venture gasping through the granite air,
A sickly wanderer, Cain's heir: *Where shall
I go?* I crave the nooks and coves, the wooded
Glens and amber light of Devon — I must see
Some outdoor beauty, or my mind will die —

Anonymous, Undated

Centuries ago, they say, in Catalonia
his Eminence, meaning to do the old man a favour,
chose not to summon one more crucifixion,
annunciation, adoration, transfiguration, resurrection,
but asked him instead to paint the grace of God.

After a month the artist, thinner, coughing,
hauled to the gates of the bishop's palace
a prospect of a girl in a green dress climbing
rough stairs in a provincial town, high above
a river where three children splash. Elms beyond them
ruffle in a breeze. The sundried square
echoes with merchants hawking wool or damsons,
ceramic dishes or newly stiffened bread.
Hopeful, scrawny as Lent, a cat complains
to a man who left the coast in darkness bearing
elvers, codfish and an air of salt.
                                        As the noise
and bustle collapse into the light, the girl
goes up the steps alone. A locket glistens
below her neck. She ignores the crimson
cyclamen spilling through a mullioned window
and the swallows bent on gathering near
the heavy tongue of a towering bell
for there – half-concealed by a pillar
at the painting's edge – a boy stands waiting.

"But what is this?" the bishop said. "I wanted –"
And the old man interrupted, "I did."

In Girona Cathedral

Even the highest, mightiest tomb will not
give permanent shelter: blond Ramon
the murdered count of Barcelona, boots
atop a spaniel, long fingers crossed in stone.

Pride forbids a lord to wait in death
below some rancid serf: he welcomes grief
or suffers scorn above a chapel door,
closer to heaven than he could leap in life.

Yet she of the floppy ears and saucer eyes
never expected resurrection: all
she knows, having dreamed the pilgrim centuries,
the tourist decades, are the weight and aim
of her armoured master's limestone legs,
back-breaking, indestructible as time.

Paradise

1

A bar in Amsterdam.

The forests of the flame-templed babbler, the Juan
Fernandez firecrown, the 'O'u.

When I was younger, you.

2

There was no Eden. Every hour was Eden.

But in the aftermath, a garden.
Lemon, thyme, ginger. Cedar, impatiens, bay.

A garden with walls, holding the world at bay.

3

Stories we recite to ease our pain

Trying to keep brushwood alight in the rain,
Hellfire missiles, sabre cats or AK-47s

Determining the lie of heaven.

A View of Delft

"…a special place not in his own time, when he was ignored, but outside it. Vermeer has taken his place in the history of the taste of the last hundred years, and from the strictly historical point of view he should hardly be mentioned."

The town blew up in 1654
killing several friends and his wife's relations
and his painting master: a powder magazine
exploded without warning, for secret reasons
perhaps a function of the recent war
or a prospect of the one to come.
All over Delft the dogs and birds
kept silent for a minute,
as though respectful of the dead or shocked
at the ashen light above. The trees
had lost their yellow leaves
by the time the fires burned out
and a moon appeared in blue. Its filmy
image in the river was enough
to illuminate parts of bodies
and furniture that had not sunk.
    His wife was buying cheese and fish
in the market: she stumbled home
with a splinter of oak embedded in a cheek,
the remnant of a flying stall.
They were two of the lucky.
In a garret he had been examining
a Spanish painting: two remorseful saints
and a stubbled Christ who fell
from his arms to the checkered floor.
    How had this come to pass?
A state inquiry found nothing
and many citizens, kept in the dark,
nurtured a dark suspicion
they feared to speak aloud. The ruins
became a coy attraction for outsiders,

Mark Abley

grateful to God that such a calamity
had left them free to go their ways unhindered
by conscience or the need to build.
    In June he wandered
through the snarled remains, watching
a pair of black and scarlet songbirds
foreign to the town in former days
nesting in the rubble of a merchant's wall.
A day of storm and sunlight,
the ground as firm as risen bread:
from across the river, the houses
were likely to stand forever. When will
the next explosion come? That evening
a girl he knew in one of those houses,
its brickwork warm as milk,
gave birth to an eyeless,
armless boy, dying in a puddle
of her own dark blood,
the surgeons helpless and ashamed.

Fire

*"We scorched and boiled and baked to death more people in Tokyo
that night of May 9–10 than went up in vapor at Hiroshima and Nagasaki."*
— Gen. Curtis LeMay

Sixty years later, when the rain has dwindled
and darkness has pacified the baritone crows,

a Tokyo sky mutates into trembling
scrolls and screens, a calligraphy of fire,

the planet Saturn, snails, a weeping willow,
childish faces with eyes that linger an extra

second, two heads of cats, a geodesic dome
inside a heart that morphs into a galaxy

as the watching girls in flip-flops and kimonos
and a few of their t-shirted boyfriends *ooh* and *aah*,

the crackle of a dozen explosions peeling
clouds above the harbour into blood orange juice;

I nibble an octopus roll and sip Pocari Sweat,
wisps of purple smoke playing hide-and-seek among

the towers as I brush against a man in the crowd,
his wiry, salt-coloured hair at my shoulder;

How, I want to ask, *did you manage to live
when the sky delivered fire that broke your city,*

*frying infants on their mothers' backs,
boiling children alive in the canals, killing*

a hundred thousand people in a night...but I don't
speak his tongue; and the old man is beaming.

　　　　　　Mark Abley

Poppy Men

1

I watch them stride across my childhood:
ramrod, beribboned, glancing
over the assembled school as if our chatter
failed to scuttle something I never
heard or glimpsed in Hogan's Heroes, men
as young as my black-haired mother.

2

Six were left from some ancient war,
six and then five who could picture
the veldt, five and then four who had bled
for Victoria, marched to Pretoria, four
and then three at the pale stone slab
with its metal flowers, three and now —

3

Now this: a man who liberated
Holland in a strip mall, his chair between
Photo Quick Kims and Quincaillerie Steve,
accosting no-one, troubling a few
November shoppers by his wordless gaze
as if we might imagine

The Next

(Madeline-Ann Aksich, 1956–2005)

One day the perennials pray for mercy from the sun;
    the next, umbrellas sprout like Portobellos.
One day the big boxes are fanfaring midsummer specials;
    the next, back-to-school sales.
One day your mother reads a novel in a corner of your left eye;
    the next is darkness.

One day the cat looms across a chair and will not budge;
    the next, he cries until nightfall in the kitchen.
One day children watch a village turn to smoke;
    the next, they learn the grammar of refugee tents.
One day the garish pills are keeping your tumours in check;
    the next, your optic nerve gets squeezed into your skull.

One day two swallows swallow June bugs, mosquitoes, midges;
    the next, a dozen gather on a copper wire.
One day you need to show ridiculous courage and you do;
    the next, the same; the next, the same.
One day you're in what people call mid-life

A Map of Grief

1

"How long since I was told," I dreamed
    a hunchbacked man was muttering,
"that somewhere in a Latin manuscript,

bound inside the leaves of a leather book
    of anatomy no-one has fingered
since a novice filed it on the highest

shelves of a monastic library
    in a city on the fringe of Europe
a good four hundred years ago,

you will find a map of grief,
    charted by a Flemish sage
who knew the genome of the heart,

each brook of loss, each berg of pain
    drawn lifelike and lifesize:
if you could trace the text

you might pass your life unfolding
    the map until it clothed the earth,
the sage's earth and yours."

2

Make it specific: ok then, the woman
    wrapped in black, walking with trees
on her back down a hill to a refugee camp
    just inside Ethiopia: three children
dead of TB, the girl at her breasts
    dying of it: the look in her eyes
as you ask for her age and name
    and write them as if you own her:
the way she does not say goodbye: the look
    you would have worn had she lingered
and a soldier from one of the district's
    dozen armies had jumped off
a stolen tank, saluted, and torn
    her face away from her skull. *Make it
specific:* but this is the species we are,
    these are the griefs we know, not least
the one that feels like sand on the roof
    of the mouth as we turn away.

3

Wipe the map clear, hide it away:
But how? And where?

Deny it, deface it, cover it up:
With what? Till when?

Eliminate it, forget about it:
Quick to say, slow to do.

Give it up, lead a normal life:
A normal life?

4

A normal life means this: you forget
   the sufferings of others
except the few you can relieve.

My advice: if you take up cartography,
   fix your mind on rainfall
or the lurching of tectonic plates.

If you must break into emotions,
   devise a graph of joy: the data
will be rare but heartfelt.

A habit of grief is the way
   it keeps growing: all over the planet
changing its walkabout shape, reforming,

deforming, weighing down nations
   and generations, adding new wrinkles,
refinements of pain, scar tissue

to mark the skirmishing ages.
   Grief patrols our faces,
it squats on our maps to laugh.

The Guangzhou Engineering Student: A Letter

Father, I am a little scared to explain
    I will not be travelling home to spend
the New Year festival with you and with my mother.
    Nothing, father, used to give me richer pleasure
than tiptoeing beside you as our kite
    floated high above your head toward the hills.
But this year, father, I cannot make
    the winter journey: her name is Lo Chung
and for seven months she has served the public
    in the Silver Palace Restaurant. Father,
you have been young, can you please imagine
    the joy of wandering a city with my friends
on a Saturday night, not discussing metallurgy
    but strolling past the neon signs of Xiajiu Lu,
the bridal parties and the Paris blouses,
    diamonds, leopard coats and golden arches
brighter than a thousand village moons?

No, my father, I do not think you can.
    If you have not already torn this page in two,
then before you read it to my mother
    can I tell you one last thing? On my birthnight
in late November, after we walked
    down Xiajiu Lu, my friends and I,
we found our bicycles and rode the streets
    to Shamian Island where my love stood working.
We dined on fresh-plucked pigeon and yellow wine
    and Lo Chung, wearing a neat dark skirt
and a jacket the colour of ripe watermelons –
    the sweet inside, I mean – smiled at me with her eyes
till all my laughing friends fell silent.

Father, have I said too much? May the year
    unfurl without me like a dragon kite.

PART
TWO

A Wooden Alphabet

My summer project is to learn the script
these withered twigs spell out against the air —
the ones that look so still, against the frantic
    bobbing of ash leaves above and below,
and their downward-spiralling keys, and the clouds
cruising past the shoreline like a toy flotilla
framed by an alphabet of naked, spindly,
            rickety wood.

It's not a fruit tree, so I can't believe
a gardener's clumsy grafting has to bear
the blame for this gnarled calligraphy. Stripped
    to the bone, these limbs resist the talons
of a great horned owl. I've heard it calling from
some leafy vantage when the light drew in,
as though to give the mice a final chance
            to flee for home.

Letters in the sky: the more you study them
hanging like a lost refrain above the lake,
the more convinced you grow of their lucidity;
    and the less certain it becomes
that such exact articulations are
nothing but the leftovers of lightning, mold
or leaf-devouring beetles. True, if you surveyed
            the pattern from

a wider angle, the shapes would alter,
the way a dialect mutates a vowel sound,
yet their branching language would remain the same:
    a skeleton in search of flesh
if not a koan waiting for a student's
enlightened yell — "It spells FRUSTRATION, yes!"
And also this: the poetry of earth
            is made of death.

Learning to Read

You don't need to grasp the meaning
   of the taut, precise Inuktitut script
to catch the drift of this primer —

a white whale blowing and snoozing,
   lunching on a school of dappled fish,
nursing a seal-sized calf — but only

a children's book that emerged from
   Kangiqsualujjuaq
might dare these last few pages:

the hooded figure in a sea-green kayak
   becomes a boy devouring chunks
of meat on a stony beach, his cheeks

packed with the animal who frolicked
   through the waters of Ungava Bay
four drawings back. On the cover

the whale, though dead, is still intact
   and a small child stands alone, arms high
above the skin as if in blessing:

Belugas are good! Welcome to land!

         Mark Abley

Flight

in the free sky above
        a combe, a coulee,
                a wadi at dawn

a song is fluttering, taking
        wing, hunting for breath,
                the spendthrift

melody lost in
        a thousand languages and
                found and lost again, always

willing to be
        discovered in raptor air
                on a limestone ridge

a delta, a muskeg,
        white spray through a salt marsh,
                in veldt and columbine

thickets, the songs are waiting
        for earth to shape them,
                bodies to wear thèm

bones to ground them
        in tooth and muscle,
                air against tongue

among the high firs, a trail
        to a waterfall, hidden
                cave at the instep

of a mountain, dark root
        in the sinews, playing
                fresh music, the nerve

Down

These are the trees chopped down, chopped in a day.
The mahogany stretches from here to St. Eustache.
Teak sprawls even farther in the opposite direction.
Oaks jostle ginkgos, figs rub up against maples,
date palms disturb the highways; the birchbark is white trash.
These are the trees chopped down, chopped in a day.

These are the trees chopped down, chopped in the night.
I never thought so many walnut logs could fit on the back
of a truck. Now nothing surprises me: not the littered olives,
not the stink of eucalyptus, not even the crumpled
mountains of bamboo. Something lived in a snarl of sumac.
These are the trees chopped down, chopped in the night.

These are the trees chopped down, chopped by the hour.
Tomorrow they'll emerge as plywood, pulp or fire.
A lifetime ago last week they sheltered rainbows in a canopy
or tangled against snow, subarctic bonsai:
willow, larch, arbutus, the chainsawed fruits of desire.
These are the trees chopped down, chopped by the hour.

Mark Abley

Into Thin Air

1

Dr. William L. Rhein of Harrisburg, deserting his *Heartbreak
Hotel* -era patients to explore an ancient vestige of
roadless forest high in the western Sierra Madre,
was aboard a mule when a single Imperial
Woodpecker clambered up a dead pine in plain view

and he filmed her foraging the scaly trunk,
chipping the bark, her black lizard-like crest
twitching before she heaved into flight,
her pointed tail disappearing
beyond his ability
to deploy a handheld
camera further:

the only day
her kind was
ever
shot

2

Chastened, wrinkled, reclusive, he likened the creature to "a great
big turkey flying in front of me," his hands quivering: now
a few clicks of my index finger revive on a screen
the ghost of a younger, butterball man in a hat
who drilled cavities to buy his Mexican trip

and reveal an almost heart-shaped whiteness in
the woodpecker's folded wings: how she'd leap
off a tree before briskly flapping
away: if the sound equipment
hadn't weighed so much, we might
still understand just what
Rhein meant by "cackling"

and "the usual
toy trumpet
sounds" she
gave

3

When biologists, half a century later, found a way back,
they discovered the loggers had left almost nothing uncut:
opium poppies grew where the opulent pines had stood:
in the minds of oldtimers the largest woodpeckers
ever to roam this planet persisted as half-

forgotten medicine, half-remembered meat
and the trusting dupes of a sawmill boss:
he paid his men to smear the doomed trees
so the birds, using their long pale
beaks to drill for larval grubs,
would ingest poison and
at a loss for breath

could prevail on
sumptuous
wings no
more

Garefowl

1

The sea was spattered with icebergs
and grim and the prize of ten shillings,
put up by the chief mate when drunk
should any man swim the breadth of the harbour,
bounced in his pocket. At seven o'clock
we sailed for the islands: three rough hours
with a dripping wind battering
storm clouds into a fleet.

The rocks inshore being spiky,
being feathered in mist, we laid anchor
and seven gunners took to the boats,
one singing *There's no discouragement
shall make me once relent...*
On the first rock my younger brother
and I discovered puffins
and gulls; and the second; the third.
But after noon on the fourth rock
I noticed two of our prey: they peered from
a ledge at us, child's play to kill.

Our meagre haul made the captain
lose his Irish temper.

And now I doubt if any remain
even on the secret islands
off the Faeroes, nor have I heard the name
spoken lately. The ship's boy
whaling last year near Tahiti
thought it a goose or duck.

Mark Abley

2

Breath clangs shut, demanding
the freedom of air in the mouth's deeps:
Gare the high beak for fishing,
Air the sacs that detained the bird two minutes
Underwater, *ir* its croak of a song.

Then the glottis hurls open the name:
a fricative presses out from its throat
before the arctic vowels whirl
down the feathers past muscle and fat:
sonority, grease, the eyes' hard flame.

The word enfolds the bird. Its foretoes
web together: two syllables, two diphthongs.
Some names – phalarope, sanderling – fly
but these black rudiments,
runt-wings, get drenched in the current.

While the pickled skin and bones
adorn museums "this most honourable
and ancient foule" lingers in its dying name.
Garefowl: night and snow, island and ocean,
one mate and one egg, one body

for all the stern winds.

3

The words breed so lustily that in less
than half an hour I filled two boats.
Inspected, rejected them all.
Some of them sidled back, whispering
I am beauteous, *take me* or
I am heavenly, *married to* hellish,
A happy compliant couple. I dumped them.

And launched a dory
for the Isle of Old Nouns,
fogbound as ever. I practised aim
on the pebbles, rolling
my tongue on their bite and sheen:
obsidian, basalt, coy *magma.*

I found the bird waiting
in the interior, sitting up straight
on a granite shelf facing me.
The white patch beside each eye
said to me *milk, ivory, salt,*
salt meat for the long winter.
The white patch said *paper,* said *cumulus
on ice.* The white patch took me
and I took the fowl
from its lair but its egg
lurched into the air.

Behind a window my booty
faded with other prizes, and now
I am letting it out to preen
its dusty extinct feathers,
tremendous under surf
till we knew the bird by name.

A Labrador Duck

"Not seen since 1875. Presumed to be extinct."
(handwritten label in the Redpath Museum, Montreal)

Presumed, indeed! It's time you changed the label —
year upon year I watch it fading and withering,
a peculiar relic in your eyes
just as I am, posing in a glass box beside
a brace of passenger pigeons, each of us
a curiosity, a brief distraction
as you trudge from dinosaur to mummy.

Sixty of my kind, I hear, were spared
the usual fate of the dead. But I imagine
their feathers too are starting to disintegrate,
the cells in their bills dissolving despite
all your efforts to render us immortal.
It doesn't work; it never works; one happy day
I expect to crumble. As for my previous life
there are many things I'm proud to say
you'll never know — our habits of courtship,
our flyways and byways, why we had so little
chance against you — and I'm not telling.

Stop. Look me over, and please let me
indulge my only pleasure: looking back at you.
Now that feeding, flying, mating and diving
are impossible, the chance to ponder you
is all I've got. Call me an anthropologist,
alert to the coded meanings in your plumage,
the significance of tiny frowns. In yarmulkes
and bobby socks, Bermudas and chadors,
Paisley shirts and leather boots that hurt the floor,
you come and go, dying slowly on the stairs.

So here I stand: preserved and catalogued and webbed,
a trophy of your deadly skill, while you –
still free to taste the wind and weather,
peering in at me as though I had the answer
to some query on the tip of your tongue –
recede into the growing past.

Mark Abley

Eurycea Tridentifera

A salamander, pink-white, found
only in Honey Creek Cave
with remnant, atrophied eyes,
its home a void of light —
should anyone care if
the slippery creature dies?

No economic value,
not the future of the genus:
one of nature's small
astonishments, a blind
perpetual swimmer with
what my *Audubon* calls

a "snout depressed abruptly"
below the dissolving bedrock,
the persimmon-dotted hills…
No telling what it perceives.
If a city drained the aquifer
or some zealot blasted the hell

out of Honey Creek and sent
its dwellers to kingdom come,
why grieve for a minute?
— Just because our spinning
earth no longer belongs
to the wild things in it

and they vanish one by one,
hour by hour, pale morsels
of flesh that can hardly dream
what the world has swallowed up
since a few intrepid ancestors
made a cave their home.

One Night

for my daughter

These clouds have made an archipelago.
    A plane is tacking through the channels of black water
as the moon, no longer round,
    glistens from a saltmarsh of the sky
like the nestled egg of some wind-erasing bird,
    a migrant from the far-flung homeland.
One night, Megan, it will hatch.

Egret Song

To step across the black, soaked sand

so lightly your feet
leave no impression

to balance on a slab of seaweed-
crusted granite where the waves
disintegrate

impossible
that legs so delicate
could bear the weight of a spine, a brain,
muscles, a stomach, a heart

your eyes as
sharp as the spikes of a sea urchin
discerning, probing

what no-one else can see before
foaming water surges

and your wings lift

One Swallow

Veering and skittering a wing's breadth above
grass and cement, indifferent to risk,
gone before an eye can follow:

are the moths and mosquitoes really so quick
you need to put on this Cirque du Soleil,
forked-tail, will-o'-the-wisp display?

Look at the managerial starlings
pecking away beneath you: don't they
make you a little envious of land?

No. Breath of sky, it's inconceivable
you should lurk in mud's element.
Blue-black wanderer, bird in no hand,

dodger, freelancer, showman, corkscrew
of air: on your swivelling travels,
never lose faith in your act.

When you hurtle south for a winter
the sky grows pale-faced and stormy without
your insouciant, whippersnap flair.

The days hunker down in your absence,
needled no longer, stolid as work. Your flight
was their thread: now you're dangling

over Guyana, still chasing lunch
with that cool improbable artlessness.
We miss you. You always missed us.

Blind, Electric

"How this came to be is a real interesting question."
— Prof. William L. Fink

Ian, give up flyfishing the upper Bow.
Leave Montana's trout streams alone.

If you parked your Honda by the Amazon
no Dolly Varden pilgrim

or rainbow partisan would wreck your solitude,
reeling as the light pours down.

"The Amazon water is muddy,"
says Dr. Fink the ichthyologist,

"and twenty feet down, it's black."
Which is why, in the deeps, creatures grow

who spend a life without light —
blind, electric animals that eat

nothing but the tails of other fish
and can, if munched, regenerate their own;

eyeless transparent catfish;
fish that devour dead wood

by the banks where you'd be standing, Ian,
casting your luck upon the waters,

listening to bossa nova in waders
and wondering how it feels to swim

through a darkness charged with currents,
taste buds all over your skin.

Zoo

The almond-eyed
wolves, the chuckwallas;
fruit bats galore;
a royal tiger pacing,
pacing; zebras, four of them
earning their stripes;
wombats, toucans
and a wallaroo;
in the night house, mouse
lemurs, almost extinct;
a pair of implausible
hoopoes above
a Manchurian boar:

Is all this not
enough for us? How can
we ask for more?

Yet we do, we do.

Mark Abley

Proofs of Loss

— Dominical, Costa Rica

At night we face the ocean looking south:
    a hood of stars, a beard of sand,
pale ropes of water lashing at our eyes.
Weakling Polaris and the Southern Cross
    drip light like ancient, dim fireflies
before thick Pacific rainclouds push inland.

We improvise a meal from yucca, beer
    and mackerel; that glint across
the surf must be a local snapper boat,
condemned a year ago. Come the next gale
    its hull will smash, and gear will float
ashore, new neighbours for these other proofs of loss:

debris of forests, rack of holidays,
    the tousled metal on the rocks.
Our camping site was once the fond escape
of some rich soul marooned in San Jose,
    for whom its walls blazed out the hope
of pleasure, sweet release, a life unruled by clocks.

Look at it now, by twitching candlelight:
    a trickling roof, three broken chairs,
the iron bed collapsed onto a floor
not swept in years. Was this the water's fault —
    long waves that undermine the door,
pressed by a current to subvert the land's affairs?

Or was the man the victim of a lie?
    Corals, dolphins, a lavish sun;
rapturous weeks of lazing on the beaches
devouring joy and daiquiris at will...
    But all his ruined schemes can teach us
is never to confuse escape with liberation.

At noon we face the ocean looking south.
    The glossy, fluid sand is blue.
A pelican skims the breakers as he flies
past a sea turtle washed up by the tide.
    White syrup has replaced its eyes.
"That smell – like addled honey – does it beckon you?"

K'tunaxa

A conversation of ravens, hurled into
      the wind as it pushes low
across the dry forget-me-not ridges,
      the green flats of the Bow,

echoes off the scree like verbs from the tongue
      of travellers who knew each gap
in the cloud peaks, harvesting the valleys,
      retreating before the snow,

verbs in a language without relatives,
      a relic on a ripped map,
mouths that possessed a word for "starving
      though having a fish trap."

PART
THREE

Mother and Son

(Lethbridge, 1964)

You are the voice in the kitchen singing;
I am the smell of new-washed linen
in a summer bedroom with the window open
before drowsiness tucks me in and silence falls.
You are the ladies' book-club member;
I am the furtive reader of *Anatomy
of a Murder*. You are the steady
towel beside the bathtub, the avid
hands that grasp a gold report card; I am
the dripping body, I am the
reported gold. You are the heavy-lidded eyes
battling tears at Mr. Abley's
new absurdity or old tirade;
I am the spiteful giggler;
together we conspire. You are
the warm front; Mr. Abley is
the cold front; I am the weather's edge.
You are the crucifix above a bookshelf;
I am the word made flesh. You
are all memory; I am
all forgetting, all struggling
to forget. You are the sleepless
presence waiting; I am an absence
waited on, moist fear withdrawing into
new-washed lemon sheets;
I overhear your love song by the counter
and my small heart thumps assent.

After Pinocchio

1

I recall the fear.

I recall the green-faced devil
who gripped Pinocchio in a fist
ready for the boiling oil.

"But now it's bedtime," I was told.
"We'll read another chapter
tomorrow. Sweet dreams, my dear."

In the wake of Sir Serpent's
lithe tongue and bloodshot eyes?
Sweet dreams, when a bearded grownup
means to roast a boy?

2

This is what happens if we lose control.
This is what happened after weeks of play.
This is what may happen to you.

He frolicked with his friends on Pleasure Island
until the day he awoke and found his ears
a furry burden on the scalp.

Then his hands and feet turned into hooves.
As he bucked with fright, his skin was hide.
A tail began to swish beside his rump.

He opened his mouth to cry in fury
but the only noise was a bray.
"This is what will happen to me,"

I felt in the darkness of my room,
"if I'm bad. It's evil to have fun.
It must be normal to obey."

3

Each time he lies, his wooden nose
  grows more and more erect.
Only if he speaks the truth
  can he enjoy neglect.

Honesty shrinks the boy's condition
  to manageable size.
The lesson: call on fantasy
  to make an organ rise.

Mark Abley

4

You're bundled into a cell.
   You flabbergast the fish offshore.

Ne'er-do-wells urge you to sin.
   Though bred like no other boy

you will die, if you must, for your father —
   such a faithful only son.

Then you'll rise again in flesh…
   Where have I read all this before?

5

To feed the moral
   the plot has to lead the child
into temptation.

If he refuses
   there might be nothing to say,
no wood to turn flesh.

6

What's true to life, I guess,
is how everyone suffers.

In the rough Italian, before
Disney smoothed the waters,
father is lost at sea.
Pinocchio kills the cricket.
The fairy dies of grief. The fox
goes lame, the cat goes blind
and Pinocchio's best friend —
young trouble who becomes a donkey —
gets beaten like a donkey.
He's a worn-out nag when he dies.

And the boy who sees all this
is a puppet. He has free will,
he thinks, the way we all do.

7

How would I rewrite the story?

Get rid of the blue fairy,
the unfortunate fox and cat.
Get rid of the knowing cricket.
Away, away with all that!

Get rid of the saltwater monster,
the reptile, the donkey boys.
Get rid of them all but Pinocchio
and multiply his joys.

Allow him his raucous innocence,
his rude brand of fun.
Allow him to keep his father
if Geppetto accepts a son

who may not follow orders
and won't be whittled away
by anyone who sees pleasure
as the herald of decay.

…Perlis, Chamba, Tannu Tuva…

I found the blue album in a crate, a relic
  of my years of pumpkin-coloured
report cards and burnt rice pudding. Some
  pages brimmed with monuments and dead men
yet the unfamiliar names on top of unfilled space
  told me nothing of the lost nations
that lurk in the wizened geography of stamp books —
  Fezzan, Ifni, North Ingermanland,
the Romanian Post Offices in the Levant…

Then I turned a leaf to an orange and white
  morsel of commerce, once licked in Afrique
Équatoriale Française: forty centimes
  to buy a stranded
rhino in a clearing, poised against the partial
  sky. A python slithers up a cluster of vines,
its head a fleshy arrow, its body
  thicker than a child's thigh. No child,
woman or man appears on the stamp, only
  these emblems of imperial glory,
the butchered wealth of Oubangui-
  Chari, the Middle Congo and Tchad.

It lay pasted alone in a corner as though
  the suburban boy expected more
from the lettered jungle or himself. Wearing
  an armour of exotic dreams
I loved my golden rhino like a buddy
  in the small, rectangular world.

The Fingerprint

Watching you, big sir, arrange your wife
   keeping Bow Falls in the middle distance
      while Cascade Mountain rises artistically behind

I remember how I used to do the same
   (minus a wife) with my first Instamatic:
      how, weeks later, my mother would carry home

a fat yellow envelope of holiday shots
   and I'd rush to my room, tearing, wanting
      the roadside glacier, conifers in dry air,

whiskeyjacks, the ice-green lake, a marmot's cry until
   I saw, one after one, my fingerprint
      in the lower right corner, the telltale whorls

below Mount Rundle, blocking the Frank Slide,
   beside the grazing head of a Waterton elk,
      obscuring my parents by the Lundbreck Falls.

Perhaps your wife, sir, is your fingerprint.
   I'm in no position to complain. I'm not
      watching Bow Falls, I'm watching you.

Oxford Sonata

The robin who kept on hurtling
the river from willow to willow
sang no louder or clearer as we
nestled on his territory. And
although he acted tamer than
a kingfisher or stoat,
even if we'd rooted crumbs
of gingerbread from our pockets
he would never have fed from our hands.
We were rocks at home in the earth,
we were stones the water
polished. When he landed so close
you could have stroked his breast
he was merely preparing a foray
into rival airspace

         — not
working to make us a couple as
bells pealed beyond the meadows,
a dog clamoured downriver, and
neither of us dared a breath —

            last
night while he must have rested
wing muscles, nerves and lungs,
I dreamt that I could sing
to you as he carelessly did,
and the smile his music conjured
out of silence grew again.

Expecting

There you are: this dome inside your mother's belly
   as she lies supine on a metal slab
and a thin technician daubs his tube of jelly

on the skin hill. His unctuous machine
   is gliding over you, translating noise
into broken light and blackness on a screen

we scrutinize to gain a primal sense
   of who you are: a curled-up shape
with a spine, a swimming head that looks immense,

femurs, a thick placenta and a host
   of qualities I strain to comprehend.
It doesn't work. All I see is a ghost.

2

The snow is melting. The snow comes back.
   Our walks are ponderous and brief.
I triple-check your future room.

A cot is ready. The clothes are clean.
   A suitcase bulges with New Age music,
sleepsuits, diapers, champagne

and still you linger in the vaulted womb,
   exclusive home, a private fief.
The snow is melting. The snow comes back.

3

A butcher, a baker, a man dressed in leather:
    for all the roles your friends might take, I know
two characters you'll never meet: your mother

and father, nibbling croissants on a cold
    March night, a comedy of expectation
in need of action. We've escaped the world:

the countless vicious things that have been done
    this week evaporate like foreign weather,
a fleeting shower beneath a far-off sun.

Each of these makeshift meals might be the last,
    stranger, before the hour you seize and shake
and burst your darkness for the stinging light.

4

So, Megan, what did you anticipate
    heading down the channel to a rim of fire,
a crowning and the arduous strait
    when your formidable shoulders bore
down through your mother's pain, her torn flesh?

Whatever your membrane-circled dreams,
    they gave no foretaste of the dropper load
of bitter vitamins, the tincture
    of iodine smeared on your stumpy cord,
the needle's thrust into a rose-red foot.

Yet as the rising moon above the city
    lit up night four, I watched you peer our way
with your remote, silver-blue eyes
    as though you'd travelled from a shadow planet
expecting us to know your cries.

White Nights

The freedom to be irresponsible...
like girls and boys who lounge above the Neva

at 1 a.m. in June, prepared for trouble,
swilling a dozen bottles of bad vodka,

exchanging licks on a guitar and laughing
at Mother Russia's broken-toothed tableau,

a Baltic wind across their shining knees.
I watch their hands and tongues discover pleasure

and jolt awake to find my daughter coughing.
Yellow crusts have glued her lids together.

She brawls for breath through a congested nose
and tiny lips whose only word is *Dada*.

Force-feeding medicine to spike her fever
I see the star-cold sky begin to glow.

Small Night Music

A man yells in the street beyond your window
where somebody is failing to park; the rain
drips off the outdoor staircase heavily
onto the earth; a siren tells of a crisis
the next road over.
                 Was it the siren
that woke you, trading the velvet breaths
of your sleep for sobs? Low, baffled
whimpers at first; then, as your dream
eludes the yellow blanket, they grow
quicker and push into cries, the kind that well up
through your neck, as though it's getting
tough to breathe.
                That's when I go in,
tugging the cord of the musical bird
for its tinny lullaby. You look up
blearily to give the tune a home. My exact
vowels and consonants don't matter.
                   And later,
when you're back on your own in a dark room,
a passing truck hurts the night
like a raw throat coughing. Somebody's feet
hit the staircase. Did the white cat sneeze?
The rain carries on like a heart.

The Not Quite Great

I think continually of those who are not quite great,
whose duties demand as much as they can give,
are in two minds, or lack the sudden courage
to shatter obligation like an egg.
Under the sun they hurry away from the sun,
knowing that in the shade a hundred tasks await them;
conscious, too, of the daily price
of poverty or laughing children or a friend
in pain. To them the small hours do not bring
a double orgasm or rum's oblivion
but a drenched diaper or an old, racked hand
they clutch and squeeze while looking through
a gap in the discreet curtains at the night.
Given a chance, they might not even want
a second chance at the careless life
but imagine it with a tense nostalgia, as though
the essential delight of their blood
were disintegrating under pressure into
shards of memory that scratch the heart.

Montreal

WE ARE A SIGN THAT ISN'T READ
A punch-drunk, dust-in-the-eye sort of day,
the city waiting with bruised lips for rain.
I wander down the Main past
the all-dressed hot dogs, a half-dressed
black girl smoking in a doorway
near the Chinese herbal shops with powdered
centipedes and gallbladders in jars before
crossing a freeway to the old quarter —

CHÉ PU OÙ CHU RENDU
A grey-stubbled man is blowing a mouth organ
between the Brewery Mission and some
vente de liquidation: the eyes in his
swaying head stay closed, blocking the gritty
light, speed merchants, passersby. He
keeps on playing Charlebois's "Lindberg,"
a tune that captured a rebel decade,
his ravaged face basking, impervious —

FARINE FIVE ROSES
Sophie? Sophie? Below the jammed basilica
of Notre Dame, the chartered streets
narrow as they dip and tumble to
the river's remnant port. Now it harbours
tourists, gluttonous for memories,
eyeing a ceramic tiger imprisoned
in a jazz bar's picture window opposite
a cactus-heart and mezcal café —

LA BELLE PROVINCE 1962

A denim-clad child, sobbing in the flea market,
stumbles off to chase a sparrow.
Who scared her? Surely not this pair
of hipsters loitering beside the license plates.
They finger the metallic past. I watch them
share a private laugh. What voyage
brought them here, innocent, bespectacled
lovers without a mark of woe?

At Midnight

– the floodlights go quiet in the park.
The rink is blackened and the last boy skating.

A retriever complains on the far side of the crescent.
How long before she hears the snowtrudge of her owners,

their breath a cloud that disappears like anger
or the nightshift clatter of a freight train hauling

metal off the island as the lights erratically
vanish from houses that have lost their colour

except for a single, green, lit-up front door? A boy lugging
helmet and skates will climb three steps, looking

back to face whatever lies behind him,
ears on fire from the February chill, turning –

Hard on You

The full moon is edging across a ridge of the Green Mountains
and a wind is rattling the Gamefisher boats by the dock.
As I stand outside a rented cottage eating
sharp Vermont cheddar on a slice of oatmeal bread
I can overhear the words in a lighted cabin
opposite: "Don't you understand you're ruining my whole summer?
Exactly the way your mother ruined my life. I am
a very smart man and I hate the way you are behaving,
Will, it's getting unbelievable, you asshole,
you're almost twelve years old and nobody would think
you're my son…" When the voice falls silent
I take a hopeless swig of beer and watch
a small winged creature battering the porch light
until the black air rings with a Debussy prelude
that Will or his father chose to bring to the lake.
And over the piano's falling chords: "You know
I'm only being hard on you because I love you."

Again

Waking for no good reason after
we have made love for the first time

in far too long, I find the air
looks pale, somehow, and the silent room

smells different, as if our slow
unexpected passion had transformed

a home; but when I reach
for water, I discover

a fat, orange, white-rimmed candle
still burning, hours later, smudge

of wax congealing on the saucer
beside the used Ohio Bluetip match,

a fire your dreaming has no need for;
I climb from the sheets and blow it out,

draft of night against my drowsy body;
that's when you shudder half-

awake, stretching an arm to clutch me;
and I want you, I want you again.

Vas Elegy

1

Flat on my back, eyes wandering the ceiling,
I'm told to place my hands behind my head.

Duty keeps me lying on a stainless bed
while the surgeon finishes two "urgent calls."

He breezes back and, grinning, shaves my balls.
"You really want a needle on each side?"

He twists the radio. Too late to hide.
I hear a woman croon *Big boy, don't cry.*

The shoulders clench. The heart speeds up. I try
to wrench my mind off what my body's feeling.

2

Dream of Bhutan, dream of deep breathing,
don't think about knife blades

or the signature that gave the hospital
the right "to dispose of all affected organs,"

dream of Mediterranean beaches, don't
think about the pain or the surgeon's little

"Huh!" Dream of dolphins, angelfish,
mermaids; no, not mermaids.

3

The wisecrack surgeon sends me home in stitches.
Codeine is dynamite with Scotch and nachos.

Cancer

The white coat was pressed and terse:
    faced with its verdict
my father straightened his suit,

his blood-linen tie, his best shoes,
    and on the appointed day,
leaving nothing disorderly,

caught a bus to Admissions,
    observing each block slip
away, the long roads of the city

where his daily pleasure
    was mordant complaint
growing, car by car, invisible

as though a distant trumpet
    had called, and his cells
alone could answer.

Into the Woods

for Kayden

      The city's racket
dwindles to mute among the aspen-guarded trails
I stroll again, slower now, the laughter of girls
erupting ahead in the cottonwood valley
      where, decades ago,
you'd linger beside the creek, its plank bridge ideal
for a game of billygoat gruff – dismal vision
never made you topple and tumble – but surely
      the path looked wider
when you rushed down it, oblivious to sumac
and slithering whitethorn, searching for the green, half-
hidden opening to a mosquito-ridden
      clearing where God knows
who raised a treehouse once, ramshackle even then,
tumbledown, though you could imagine it Sleeping
Beauty's ruined palace, just as the hefty vine
      above the water
would be Tarzan's if he'd left Jane in the jungle,
appeared in Pointe Claire and befriended a weak-lunged,
tenacious, book-loving child who had to battle
      too hard to grow up.

In Return

I come back to you
in a blue winter
bristling and wary,

like an alley cat
in the moon's night
when a door

opens to a girl
in a green shawl,
mouthing her joy

in a language that smells
foreign, touching
my matted throat

with her fingernails,
giving a meal
and a double-edged

smile that warns:
— *By leaving*
you fooled nobody

but living
free of my love,
you fail yourself.

PART
FOUR

Efenechtyd

"Land or place of the monk," you say it means
in the old language, though if robed and cowled
God-hungry men ever knew this village –
smattered houses, a stream, a whitewashed church,
a pub where drovers would recuperate,
their doomed flocks clamouring beyond the yews –
the story's lost. I imagine the name
means "hamlet in the valley near a fern-fringed
waterfall dividing the roadless wood"

where you, with luck, might hear a black grouse
drumming or glimpse a red squirrel: you, walking
at the year's turn, finding above the sheep-
coloured fields and frosted beeches a nail
of moon – call it *lleuad* in the old language.

Radnorshire

When my mother dies, the eyes of a shepherd
born in the Crimean War will die again.
No-one's left who remembers his clannish ways,
his moorland dogcalls, his turns of phrase:
nothing of him roams a working mind
except those blue, unclouded eyes she met
as she tottered along a puddle-specked lane
toward a market in the primrose season.

His names will linger, cut on a stone
up the slope from where I set fresh marigolds
on grandparents I never knew. Nearby
a baker was tidying his wife and parents,
dead within a year while the foe spoke Spanish
in the South Atlantic. "Like Job of old
in the Bible," he told me, wiping his brow,
"the slate was swept clean, you might say."

Goodsoil

(from a map of Saskatchewan)

Assiniboia Patuanak Missinipe
Nekweaga

Nameless Lake
Wapata

Virgin River
Mistatim

Plato
Unknown Lake

Endeavour Revenue Success
Rose Valley
Peerless Plenty
Paradise Hill

Fusilier Wartime Major
Lucky Lake
Livelong
Fairy Glen

Leader Vanguard
Big Muddy River
Sanctuary Unity
Charcoal Lake

Stalwart Conquest
Imperial Liberty
Crooked River
Old Wives Lake

Holdfast
Compulsion Bay

         Snare Lake
         Leech Lake
Eldorado

         Hatchet Lake

Love
         Deception Lake
Bighead
         Bitter Lake
Climax

         Bone Creek

                 Nemeiben
                 Kamuchawie
                 Misekumaw
Perdue

                 Sisipuk
Forget

The Floating World

Northwest of Saskatoon: beyond the small, composed
    Mennonite towns, I pull to a stop on a gravel
road straight and narrow as the Mennonite way

to eternal life, big sloughs on either side, coots
    and pintails swimming over their reflections,
a shimmer of wind barely troubling the new

leaves of an aspen bluff. The land's emptying out —
    a paint-stripped farmhouse by a roofless barn —
or so it seems to a driver of the floating world,

a dreamer of the flooded soil: a moment of
    carelessness behind the wheel and I could drown
in grainfields lost below meltwater and runoff...

The tires revolve and clouds of pebbles swerve
    across the rear-view mirror. In front the sky
stretches down, scraping earth, wetting a blue hand.

Driving West From Milk River

Blue, a ragged stripe of blue
in the far distance and a cord of road

hauling me towards it, a tumbledown
house by a dried-up marsh, no other home,

the sun spreadeagled across the stubble,
blue teeth in the sky's mouth, a coyote

bounding the highway, no other journey,
always blue, its gravity, its lightness, turning

slowly into mountains, thin grass disturbed
by peals of wind, a dozen black cattle

near a waterhole below a yellow slope
browsing what they can, no other life

and the blue rising closer, waiting to grasp
whatever offering I am.

Mark Abley

Kicking Down Mount Rundle

Loose rock on the high face:
    the treeline is a rumour underfoot:
        each step, a ginger torture for the knees.

On the high face, loose rock:
    even the big stones bounce and skitter:
        the dust you arouse turns to smoke in the wind.

High face, rock on the loose:
    our fingers dwarf the campion:
        a cloud is wandering past my feet.

In a Desert

What we pay, Professor Juanita Fletcher starts
        to decipher, letter
by letter, from a slice of clay that her men unearthed
        as the sun rose
on the rubble of a wall beside a leather sandal,
        two carved cats,
brooches, rivets, some small change, *What we pay in this*
        – and her eyes
flicker up to a mirage of road, marauding horsemen,
        barley meadows,
a witch in a cloud of blowing topsoil, and the fear
        of dying so
far from the empire's troubled heart – *What we pay in*
        this world. Explain.

Gloria (from Asian Mass)

1

Three days after dysentery
   I rose above Isfahan

And clambered to a fire-temple
   halfway up the sky
perched on the brink of a desert
   of salmon-coloured stones
and not a tree in sight

Climbed past hawks and bee-eaters
   rolling through the air
toward a dream of flight

Where the city greens in the sun
   its leaves a crowd, a bustle
hidden from the streets
   by brown efficient walls

Three days after dysentery
   half the burning world
swims away like a carp
   through the blue pool of a mosque,
the monuments and Mazdas
   a host of shapely bubbles

These birds play like fire
   their smoking orange feathers
a gift in the breeze: they lift
   the air about them

These birds are silent riddles
   my body could die away
could jettison itself
   faint, a mote on the wind
floating in the sun's eye

To drift on a bed of water
   of golden fish and flame
a mirror implanted in the earth
   scooping up the sky
a mirror to the nest of light

The city of Isfahan
   three days after dysentery
is a riot of shining birds
   a reflection from on high

2

A blind man calls you to prayer,
Shah Abbas, sumptuous lord,
builder of half the world:
even builders have to pray.

Only the blind can mount
a minaret without danger
of poring over your harem,
hundreds of bored women

not to mention boys.
For what can you ask of God?
Not wealth, not power, not taste —
more children to kill?

more slaves to castrate?
I know, these are the shadows
in a luminous career
and scholars are enchanted

by the bridges, mosques, bazaars
made to your fluent wish —
faience and arabesque,
such pious elegance — but where

are you? Wandering disguised
among the hammersmiths and weavers,
insisting that tired ears
be charmed by running water;

master of nuance and scalpel;
carpeted, rampant, invisible.
Your glory is a mirror:
it turns you to air.

3

Five times a day the men
of Isfahan kneel down
facing Mecca on a rug
the slim hands of children
or a woman made for months

and touch their brows to wool
from the flanks of mountain sheep
combed and spun and dyed
crimson for joy, or green
as the jerkin of Muhammad

now a trelliswork of roses
and geometric leaves
intertwined like fingers
that shun the swirling dust
and the wildfire sparks of water

a basin of wet sun
behind the backs of men
imploring God the merciful
to grant the liberation
of Iran from the ungodly:

the ache for righteous vengeance
a function of the passion
that flourishes on carpets
wearing thin as patience
five times a day, for ever.

Mark Abley

4

John Foster Fraser,
cycling round the world,
1897

leaving that inscription,
a calling card or poem,
on a lion at Persepolis

when my grandmothers were children
among elderflower and rabbits
on a green small island

a thousand miles from purdah,
did you make it
home? Did you scratch your three names

all over the globe?
Did you lope through Persia
like a conquering centaur,

John Foster Fraser the Great?
Did you suffer from saddlesores
and existential doubt?

Did you ever bring to mind
these kings and sovereign carnivores
graciously bleeding in the sand?

Did you dream of the road,
the moon, a jagged desert
or the piebald landscapes in your eye?

Did you notice the poor?
Did you learn their mutual language?
Did you file reports from wherever

to wherever? Did you stop to wonder
why this silent bumpy
wayfaring made you so proud

to contemplate the past with a knife?
John Foster Fraser, did you wonder?
John Foster Fraser, could you stop?

5

Look at this Persian miniature:
a potter in a silver robe
whose hands rise up to smash
another bowl of failure.

The shards in front of his ankles
flow away, a jagged river
dammed by the silver frame
while his cloak, as though of clay,
mingles with the fragments of
a month at work.

Nothing he has fashioned is
worthy to remain
intact: only the artist
exalted in destruction.

The beauty of these pots, he thinks,
has nothing in common
with the life that swirls around me,
patched and cracked and dirty.

They were not made to function,
merely to be admired.

I will ask the man who painted
this scene to chuck it out.

Credo (from Asian Mass)

I believe in "Quite Cool Refrigeration"
   the latest hope for Lahore
when eggs would fry on the pavement
   and journalists are flogged in public:
"Pakistan is an ideological state
   with ideological frontiers"
plus a long border with India
   plus water buffalo knowledgeably
wandering the streets by themselves
   past beds on a roadway, sleepers
with no bed on a roadway
   past ancient cars and chariots
past a mosque where men lie down
   to dream in the shade
of a market: jewellery and silk
   ironware and Allah

I believe in the Ideal Book House
   "Latest books for all sexes and all tastes"
and in *Jubilate Agno*
   my birthday gift to me
"For there is a traveling for the glory of God
   without going to Italy or France"
For there is a cockroach, Christopher Smart,
   the size of a holy kitten
on my wall and I shall kill it

I believe in the noise of Pakistan
   men hawking up their phlegm
from undernourished throats
   and in the silence of Pakistan
men rolling the phlegm on their tongues
   preparing to spit
I believe in my greasy body
   and I strongly believe in water

Mark Abley

the dangerous ambrosia
   though I have my doubts about Multan mangoes
"They are the finest in the country
   and you will come to Multan
you will stay there in my house"
   "But this is not the mango season
why should you bother foreigners?"
   "Sir, nevertheless
you will come to Multan"

I want to believe in Harappa
   ruined city of an early empire
its ramrod streets baked in brick
   four thousand years ago,
its ivory seals and weights and toys
   resurrected under glass
near a complex of extravagant mounds
   "largely wrecked," an archaeologist says,
by "extraction of bricks as ballast
   for the Lahore-Multan railway"

I believe in beggars
   hard at work on a train
while the travellers wash their skins
   with fists of sand and pray
down the aisles they come, the blind
   down the aisles, a hydrocephalic
boy and his loud mother
   down the aisles, the agile
legless, the armless
   down the aisles, a
man with half a face:
   no left eye, no left ear
half a mouth, half his nostrils
   and down from his scalp to his shoulder

hang shopping bags of flesh
   I believe in you
you take my breath away
   you will not take my money
I hate your faith in charity
   and yes, I hate your face
spare me your professional hope
   spare me your mockery

I have faith in the hidden minarets
   of Shah Jahangir's tomb
green and pleasant beyond the river
   notice the elegant dome
cleverly, cleverly concealed
   and the huddle of violent flowers
the parrots and the vultures
   "This country is no good:
everyone have no money"

I believe in gaudy rickshaws
   brighter than silk and saffron
in all the puny businesses
   the rice the children gobble
the turbulence of being
   a citizen of Lahore
the refusal to lie down
   in the streets at night and die
the refusal to sink a knife
   in the throat of a stingy foreigner
full of doubts and poetry
   what use is that to you?

I believe in a skinny horse
    the colour of burnt almonds
frying in the noonday sun
    its front legs shackled together
why? but why?
    a boy explained: "a zebra"
as it hobbled down the path
    silent and determined
knowing its destination
    had nothing to do with me
why? but why?
    who possessed it
with all its face intact

Amdo, 1938

"It was a house, I recall, below a cedar hill
with a spotted mastiff in the yard and juniper
waterspouts protruding from the roof.
We felt anxious that a meddlesome warlord
had sent spies, and more anxious, to be candid,
in case the oracles had spoken falsely
and the omens would prove untrue."

    In a nation of wild strawberries and liquid butter,
    of bones exposed among the ice-blue passes.
    Nation of incense, gold and grief.

"I disguised my priesthood in a servant's robe:
the crows were singing as we left the path.
In the windowless eastern wall there was a door
and behind the door, a little boy
impatiently awaiting us. He had been born,
his mother said, in a stable – a detail
no-one was expecting in the capital."

    In a nation of blood pheasants and woolly hares,
    of prayers that coax a blessing from the wind.
    Nation trembling on a foreign lip.

"How could my heart keep still? I was mindful
of a silver dragon twining round the teapot.
The child, as he reached for an ivory drum,
addressed us in our proper dialect
and we knew the searching years were done.
We offered him his own possessions:
tender glory; ocean of wisdom; Dalai Lama."

Lhasa, 1950

1

You had a month to play with kites,
a season to play with water
and a night when statues of butter
stood frozen on a passing street.

You had a government that banned
football and mahjong
and a people who'd obey.

You had a market where the rich
and their retinue could buy
the fresh forbidden meat,
Bing Crosby's latest disc,
silk scarves to give away.

2

Only 12,000 feet in the air,
nomads found the summer heat
too intense to bear.

If they turned from their slow advance
out of the forbidding city,
the golden roofs of a palace
disturbed the passing sky.

They would rescue
a fly who sank into their tea
in case he was your grandmother, reborn.

She was lately fed to the crows.
The butter lit her soul.

3

You had a shrine where mice of honour
could pass along a silken curtain
and flounce across the floor
to gorge on flour and butter.

You had a boy who longed to know
theology, algebra, astronomy
and the limits of his power.

You had a land in "the age of darkness"
unused to suicide or traffic
and its prayer wheels turned like the sun,
faithful revolutions
yet the mountains were unmoved.

Tibet, 1959 –

1

Imagine the monks of Ganden or Tsurphu
  had glimpsed the future of their snow-bright land:
battling to discipline a blurred despair
  they strewed a floor with multicoloured sand
and charcoal, gypsum, pollen, powdered bark,
  sprinkling a symmetry so finely grained
the wheel of time revolved within their sight,
  a funnelled grace against a charnel ground.

Kailas, if mountains had a voice, might say
  devastation is a moment's work:
a culture raped, its monasteries gutted,
  a people groping in the friendless dark.
The charnel ground has bulged to fill a nation.
  Its dead-eyed owners boast of liberation.

2

Imagine the m   Tsurphu
   had gli   ed the futu   ir sn   -b   d:
battl
   th
a   ed bark,

the wh   sight,
                        st a charnel ground.

Kailas, if mountains   , might say
   deva   ent's work:
a   asteries gutted,

      charnel gr   a nation.
      dead-eyed owners bo   f liberation.

3

Imagine the m   Tsurphu
   had gli   ed the futu   ir sn   -b   d:
battl *everything under heaven is in utter chaos*
   th *the situation is excellent*
a *power grows out of the barrel of a gun*   ed bark,
   historical experience is written in iron and blood
the wh *a revolution is not a dinner party* sight,
                          st a charnel ground.

Kailas, if mountains   , might say
   deva *the minority yields to the majority* ent's work:
a *slow growth equals stagnation* asteries gutted,
      the People's Liberation Army — that Great Wall of steel
      charnel gr *to get rich is glorious*   a nation.
         dead-eyed owners bo   f liberation.

Glasburyon

Shakespeare was an upstart, Dante a dabbler
compared to Shamil Bakhtasheni,
he of the snowpeak sagas, the quince-blossom lovesongs
and a leopard's argument with God. Not a word
of his work was dipped in printer's ink
and most of it is long forgotten;
little wonder, for the master lived
and died in the Artchi tongue, spoken
in a single windburnt village where
Dagestan falls towards the sea. The language
pleasured Shamil like a lover, giving him
poetry without an alphabet, listeners
without a page. His grave is rumoured to lie
among the roots of an apricot tree
on the scarp of a Caucasian mountain
where, if you believe the villagers, once
a month the wind recites his lyrics.

2

She flew from Boston to Port Moresby
for this: an outboard ferry ride

past a dripping wall of trees
to a yet unstudied village where

the Mombum language survives;
the wall splits open; she clambers out

and strides from the dock, escorted
by a flock of blue-winged parrots

to find the gathered islanders
seated on the red soil beside

a reed-thatched bar, watching *Fatal
Attraction* on satellite TV.

3

Reason tells me it doesn't matter
if the final speaker of Huron
goes grey in a suburb of Detroit
where nobody grasps a syllable
of his grandmother's tongue.

Reason tells me it's not important
if Basque and Abenaki join
the dozens of unproductive
languages lately disposed of; what's
the big deal, where's the beef?

Reason is scavenging the earth.
"More, more," it cries. You can't tell it
to use imagination. You can't
ask it to stop and listen
to the absence of Norn.

4

Tega du meun or glasburyon,
  kere friende min —
"If you take the girl from the glass castle,
  dear kinsman of mine,"

so a voice claims in a Norn ballad,
plucked by a rambling scholar
off the lips of a toothless crofter

he found on a Shetland island
in 1774; soon the language
was a mouthful of placenames —

yamna-men eso vrildan stiende
  gede min vara to din.
"As long as this world is standing
  you'll be spoken of."

5

That music? It's only
     wind bruising the chimes
          in a crystal fortress
               high on Mount Echo.

Each time we lose a language,
     the ghosts who made use of it
          cast a new bell.

The voices magnify. Soon,
     listen, they'll outpeal

     the tongues of earth.

Some notes on the poems

"Garefowl" was written for Anne Szumigalski, and is published now in her memory. "Labrador" is for Ann Beer; "Flight" for Brian Bartlett; "Blind, Electric" for Ian Pearson; "The Floating World" for J. Frank Roy.

"Chauvet:" a cave in the Ardèche region of southern France that holds an astonishing array of wall paintings. They may well be more than 30,000 years old.

"Labrador:" the earliest-known ceremonial burial in all of North America took place near what is now an unpaved road leading down to the coastal hamlet of L'Anse Amour.

"Deep Gold:" the originals can be found in *The Parting Light: Selected Writings of Samuel Palmer*, edited by Mark Abley (Manchester: Carcanet Press, 1985).

"A View of Delft:" the epigraph comes from Christopher Wright's *Vermeer* (1976).

"Fire:" the epigraph appears in Robert B. Edgerton's *Warriors of the Rising Sun: A History of the Japanese Military* (1997); Gen. LeMay planned the Tokyo raid. Pocari Sweat is a type of sports drink.

"The Next:" Madeline-Ann Aksich founded and directed the International Children's Institute.

"Into Thin Air:" Dr. Rhein's footage of the Imperial Woodpecker, taken in 1956, can easily be found on YouTube. A paper about the now extinct bird and Rhein's trip to Mexico, written by Martjan Lammertink *et al.*, appeared in 2011 in *The Auk 128* (4), pp. 671-677.

"Garefowl:" a vanished name for the great auk.

"Blind, Electric:" Dolly Varden is a type of freshwater char.

"K'tunaxa:" the language formerly known as Kootenai. Once spoken on both sides of the Rocky Mountains, it is now severely endangered.

"The Not Quite Great:" a riposte to Stephen Spender's "The Truly Great."

"Montreal": this poem alludes to and briefly quotes both William Blake's "London" and Robert Charlebois's song "Lindberg" (1968).

"Efenechtyd:" the old language is Welsh.

"Goodsoil:" the entire poem, including the title, consists of Saskatchewan place names.

"Gloria" and "Credo:" the long suite from which these poems are taken, "Asian Mass," evokes overland travel from Turkey to India. I made the journey as a student in 1978, the last year of the Shah's rule in Iran; by the time the poem was drafted, Ayatollah Khomeini had taken power.

"Amdo, 1938:" Amdo is the northeastern region of Tibet, better-known today under a Chinese name.

"Lhasa, 1950:" inspired by Heinrich Harrer's book *Seven Years in Tibet*.

"Tibet, 1959 – :" Both Ganden and Tsurphu monasteries were destroyed in the early years of the Chinese occupation. Kailas is the most sacred mountain in Tibet. In the third section, the italicized lines come from Mao Zedong (octet) and Deng Xiaoping (sestet).

"Glasburyon:" Shamil Bakhtasheni is fictitious, but the fate of Artchi, Mombum, Huron and Norn is not. The italicized lines of Norn are taken from "Orkney and Shetland Norn," an essay by Michael Barnes that appeared in *Language in the British Isles* (ed. Peter Trudgill, 1984). I'm happy to know this poem has been translated into Esperanto and Jèrriaise.

Acknowledgements

The majority of poems in this book previously appeared in the collections *Blue Sand, Blue Moon* (Cormorant Books, 1988), *Glasburyon* (Quarry Press, 1994), and *The Silver Palace Restaurant* (McGill-Queen's University Press, 2005). Many of the poems, especially the earlier ones, have undergone significant changes since their first appearance.

In order to republish the following poems from *The Silver Palace Restaurant*, I wish to thank McGill-Queen's University Press: "After Pinocchio," "The Fingerprint," "Blind, Electric," "K'tunaxa" (formerly entitled "Kootenai"), "Again," "White on White," "Cancer," "Vas Elegy," "Kicking Down Mount Rundle" (formerly entitled "Kicking Down the Mountain"), "Birth," "At Midnight" (formerly entitled "A Key that Opens on the Night"), "Oxford Sonata," "Eurycea Tridentifera," "The Guangzhou Engineering Student: A Letter," "Flight," "A Labrador Duck," "One Night." These poems are used by permission of the publisher.

Some of the other poems – ones that until now have not appeared in book form – first saw the light of day in the *Times Literary Supplement, Queen's Quarterly, Malahat Review, Literary Review of Canada, New Quarterly, Prairie Fire* and *CV2*. I am grateful to the editors.

I'm particularly grateful to Coteau Books for taking on this project, and to Elizabeth Philips for her keen-eyed editing. The book has been much improved by her smart, incisive comments.

About the Author

John Mahoney

Mark Abley is a Canadian poet, journalist, editor and non-fiction writer. He has published three previous books of poetry, two children's books and several works of non-fiction. He has won Canada's National Newspaper Award for critical writing and received a Guggenheim Fellowship for research into language change.

Born in Warwickshire, England, he moved to Canada as a small boy, won a Rhodes Scholarship from the University of Saskatchewan and has been a contributing editor of both *Maclean's* and *Saturday Night* magazines, and a regular contributor to the *Times Literary Supplement*. For sixteen years he worked as a feature writer and book-review editor at the *Montreal Gazette*. He lives in Montreal.

ENVIRONMENTAL BENEFITS STATEMENT

By printing this book on FSC-certified recycled paper,
COTEAU BOOKS
ensured the following saving:

Fully grown trees	Litres of water	Kg of solid waste	Kg of greenhouse gases
.44	1 608.44	24.36	63.33

These calculations are based on indications provided by the various paper manufacturers.

 Manufactured at Imprimerie Gauvin
www.gauvin.ca

MIX
Paper from responsible sources
FSC
www.fsc.org
FSC® C100212

Printed in August 2015
by Gauvin Press,
Gatineau, Québec